I0568362

THE NIGHT SEASON

Unlocking the Mystery of Your Dreams

DR. DE'ANDREA MATTHEWS

The Night Season
Copyright © 2022 by De'Andrea Matthews

Published by:
Claire Aldin Publications
P. O. Box 453
Southfield, MI 48037
www.clairealdin.com

Library of Congress Control Number: 2022931833

ISBN 978-1-954274-09-9 paperback
ISBN 978-1-954274-10-5 eBook

Printed in the United States of America.

*In **The Night Season: Unlocking the Mystery of Your Dreams**, Dr. Matthews curated heaven's guide for understanding the dream realm in a powerfully creative and spiritually provoking way. A walking classroom, Dr. Matthews delivered undeniable wisdom, unyielding spiritual proficiency, and innovated a must-read empowerment tool for every believer, especially the dreamer. **The Night Season** will inevitably expose and dismantle dark forces hidden and at work in the subconscious, activate a God-inspired dream experience, and guide readers through a compelling journey of spiritual and mental awakening and wellbeing.*

~Dora N. Watkins,
Doctoral Student & Research Scientist
University of Illinois at Urbana-Champaign
School of Social Work

Dr. De'Andrea Matthews has produced perhaps the most essential, amazing and inspiring book on interpreting dreams and visions the body of Christ has yet to read. **The Night Season: Unlocking the Mystery of Your Dreams** *will help you get clear revelation on what "thus saith the Lord" in the night hours, as well as what God is speaking to you in open visions. This may be the masterpiece of all of her books to date because it teaches you how to hear the voice of God through images and symbols. Thank you, Dr. Matthews, for blessing the body of Christ with a must-read milestone on visions and dreams for generations to come.*

~Michael C. Robinson, Senior Pastor
Ypsilanti Community Church

Dedication

This book is dedicated to my husband, Brian A. Matthews, the one who stayed up night after night, watching to make sure I slept well during my personal bouts with night terrors and anxiety. In the beginning, Brian didn't understand what I tried to explain delicately, but he soon got the revelation — firsthand. Not only does he believe that these supernatural experiences exist, but Brian has become my biggest supporter and encourager for assisting others in healing from trauma. With the direction of the Holy Spirit and the support of my husband, I am no longer afraid.

Special Acknowledgment

Thank you, Lord, for granting me knowledge, wisdom, and insight into the mysteries of the spirit realm and the kingdom of God. I am grateful that You have entrusted me with this ministry and the responsibility of teaching it to others. I count it an honor to blaze a path for the people of God to feel comfortable talking about their dreams and embracing dream interpretation as a viable method of communication to hear from You. No longer will we hide in the shadows, being concerned about what *others* may say or think. The time is now.

Table of Contents

Foreword

Dr. De'Andrea Matthews' prolific insight has truly tapped into something of highest necessity. In this book, she not only makes the case that dreams are an overlooked way that God speaks to us, but also helps us—the readers, learn how to receive those messages.

If you've been asking yourself, "Why do I keep having this dream?" or "Is this God speaking or me?", then you've found a great resource. If you're a dreamer, after reading *The Night Season*, you will be better equipped to leverage those dreams into a blueprint for your success. *The Night Season: Unlocking the Mystery of Your Dreams* will help you put your nightmares to bed and live out the plan that God has for you.

~Pastor Keenann R. Knox, Senior Pastor
Impact Church

Preface

I lived in constant fear.

I used to jump up in the middle of the night, terrified at the thought of an intruder being in the house to harm me or my children. I dreaded waking up to find that our belongings had been ransacked. I used to lie awake contemplating what all needed to be done to pay the bills, to keep the utilities out of shut-off status and not wake up to an empty spot where our only transportation was previously parked.

One particular night, the experience I had only confirmed that checking to make sure the doors were locked at night no longer mattered. The demonic manifestation that I encountered was not contained by doors or stopped by locks. Right before I woke up from a dream, I felt an excruciating pain. There was a physical presence over me, although it was invisible to my natural eyes. Struggling to get up from my bed, I turned the bedroom light on, waking my husband up in the process, only to find out that I was *not* imagining things. I had literally been attacked by a dark presence in my bedroom and had the physical evidence to prove it.

The pain that I felt was a stabbing pain, like a knife was being pushed under my thumbnail. When I looked at my thumb, it was bruised and bleeding in the *exact spot* where I felt the pain in my dream. My thumb nail remained black and bruised for more than a week, which served as a constant reminder of what I had been through in the middle of that night.

I wish that was my only experience with demonic manifestations initiated while I was asleep, but it wasn't. On a different occasion years later, I dreamed that a demonic entity was holding my ankle down. I awoke with the fingerprints around my ankle in the same place where I felt it in my dream.

I learned to handle my stress and anxiety in the same way that I had learned to navigate my dreams — to write it down and figure out the root. My personal dream journey began at about four years old, the age where I started remembering my dreams. I had a consistent, recurring dream that terrified me, though it was only darkness with geometric figures and lines. Those figures and lines represented a surgery taking place that was quite intricate, and I was unable to complete the task in the timeframe given.

My childhood home was not a Christian one; dreams were used to play lottery numbers. Instead of interpreting dreams the way God intended, my family looked to dream books like the *Kansas City Kitty* and *Three Wise Men* to determine the three and four-digit numbers they were going to play in the lottery each day.

Around age fifteen, I began my own version of dream interpretation. Still not officially introduced to Jesus Christ as my Lord and Savior, I didn't know yet that God could speak to you through your dreams. I started figuring out what certain dreams and symbols meant in my own life. *Déjà vu* or having "seen this before" kept me from being in a car accident. My mother drove that night instead of me, a young inexperienced driver. So when the tire on the car blew out on an exit with a sharp turn, she was much better equipped to safely guide the vehicle to the side of the freeway.

Figuring out early on that I needed to record my dreams, I used my diary early on and then only sparingly. I wanted to write everything down and look for patterns, but I knew better. If it was written down, it wasn't safe or private. Prying eyes were always lurking; I cringed at the thought of being embarrassed by the things experienced during my dream state. It was many years later when dream journaling became a consistent habit.

Now that I am a Christian and have learned how to seek revelation from the Holy Spirit, dreaming is much more enjoyable. The fear I experienced as a child was a tactic of the enemy to make me respond in fear, make an inner vow or not want to dream at all. That would have kept me from receiving the revelation that God has shared with me during the various phases of learning about dreams, dream interpretation, spiritual warfare and deliverance. I'm grateful for my journey; but I'm more excited to share what I've learned with you so you, too, can experience victory in your own life.

~Dr. De'Andrea Matthews

Introduction

Dream interpretation is the process of assigning meaning to dreams. We assign meaning to symbols from childhood, thus emphasizing the fact that we often have personal meanings to objects that may differ from others in our household and in our community at large. *The Night Season: Unlocking the Mystery of Your Dreams* provides dreamers with specific detailed information on figuring out what your dreams mean, whether the dreams are based on your personal assignment of meaning to symbols, the enemy's deception in what a dream actually means or the message that God is trying to communicate to you.

Another huge part of unlocking the mystery of dreams is learning how to discern the voice of God from other sources. *The Night Season* explores three sources of dreams and discusses the various forms of interference that can shift the dream and the message it brings.

Finally, it has been debated whether or not there are biblical examples of God speaking to His people via dreams. This book provides multiple, clear examples from the Holy Scriptures that demonstrate God speaking to individuals, even some popular Bible stories that we may be familiar with, but did not know that it took place while the person was asleep. If God cannot get your attention during the waking hours, He will speak to you during the night season through your dreams.

Stop treating your dreams like junk mail! While you are sleeping, your guard is down; therefore, God whispers in your spiritual ears. He's not the only one trying to capture your attention; so do not dismiss the dream realm. It represents important messages from the spiritual realm that can impact your life and your destiny.

By faith we understand that the universe was created by the word of God, so that what is seen was not made out of things that are visible.
Hebrews 11:3 ESV

My eyes are awake before the watches of the night, that I may meditate on Your promise.
Psalm 119:148 ESV

CHAPTER ONE

WHAT IS THE NIGHT SEASON?

During the *night season,* or the watches of the night, many people dream while others are awakened from their sleep, often without a clue as to why or what they should be doing. As mentioned in Psalm 119:148, as believers, right before you lay your head down to sleep at night, you should meditate on the promises of the Lord. In order to meditate or digest the spiritual nourishment of the Word, you must first read it and know what it says. Before we study what the Bible has to say about dreams, let's look a little closer at the night season. The night season is all about *intercession.*

THE NIGHT WATCHES

There are eight prayer watches, which cover the twenty-four hours of the day. Each one is divided into three-hour intervals. The twelve hours of "darkness," from when the sun goes down until the sun comes up the next morning, are the focus of *The Night Season.* These four watches are referred to as "the night watches."

Ezekiel 33 makes mention of a watchman on the wall. The military watch involves a changing of the guard. During the night season, if the church could unify under a strategic vision for prayer, taking a three-hour watch consistently, then the church would be bombarding heaven with what the Lord has already decreed, thus bringing His will to the earth. It's important to pray the Word and not our emotions or fears because heaven responds to the Word of God. God watches over His Word to perform it.

"You are right," the LORD said, "and I am watching to see that my words come true."
Jeremiah 1:12 GNT

According to Genesis 1:5 and Genesis 1:31, the day starts in the evening.

God called the light Day, and the darkness he called Night. And there was evening and there was morning, the first day.
Genesis 1:5 ESV

And God saw everything that he had made, and behold, it was very good. And there was evening and there was morning, the sixth day.

Genesis 1:31 ESV

In both Scriptures from Genesis above, evening is mentioned first and then morning, indicating that evening comes first. In the prayer watches listed below, you will notice that they begin with the first watch starting at 6 p.m. in accordance with how God established the time(s) of day.

1. The First Watch or Beginning – starts at sunset/sundown (6 p.m. until 9 p.m.)

Arise, cry out in the night, at the beginning of the night watches! Pour out your heart like water before the presence of the Lord! ...
Lamentations 2:19 ESV

2. The Second Watch or Middle Watch – (9 p.m. until midnight)

This has been referred to as "the womb" of the night watch, when evil seeds are planted against the righteous. Intercession is to prevent the evil seed from ever being planted or taking root.

So Gideon and the hundred men who were with him came to the outskirts of the camp at the beginning of the middle watch, when they had just set the watch. And they blew the trumpets and smashed the jars that were in their hands.
Judges 7:19 ESV

3. The Third Watch or Morning Watch (midnight to 3 a.m.)

And the next day Saul put the people in three companies.
And they came into the midst of the camp in the morning watch and struck down the Ammonites until the heat of the day. And those who survived were scattered, so that no two of them were left together.
1 Samuel 11:11 ESV

4. The Fourth Watch – (3 a.m. until 6 a.m.)

And in the fourth watch of the night he came to them, walking on the sea.
Matthew 14:25 ESV

HOW TO RECOGNIZE IT

When you find yourself waking up in the middle of the night, it's the first sign that you are being called to receive message from the spirit realm. Intercession means to stand in the gap to pray for someone else. Messages of intercession allow you to stand between God and mankind by engaging the spiritual realm on someone else's behalf. If you do not know what to pray, simply pray that God's will be done in their lives.

A lot of times, the enemy is seeking to disrupt God's will for that person through fear, intimidation and other tactics. Therefore, it is important that you do not conduct warfare out of fear. You cannot use the enemy's tactics (fear is one of them) to do God's work. *"For God has not given us a spirit of fear, but of power and of love and of a sound mind"* (2 Timothy 1:7 NKJV). You also must be in a place of being free from the very thing you are praying about or against. For example, you cannot pray for someone to be delivered from suicidal thoughts if you are not free from the bondage of those thoughts yourself. Pray from an understanding of the authority that you have been given in the spirit realm by Jesus Christ. Christ gives us this authority and we gain new levels of power based on what we have overcome ourselves. What we overcome becomes a part of our testimony, which serves as encouragement to others who have yet to be delivered.

And they overcame him by the blood of the Lamb and by the word of their testimony...
Revelation 12:11a NKJV

There are things at work in the spirit realm that we cannot physically see with our eyes, but it can be spiritually discerned. Keep this in mind as you learn more about the night season and how God chooses to speak to you.

BIBLICAL DREAM LEGACY

So, what does the Bible have to say about dreams? When it comes right down to it, one third of the Bible is about dreams and visions. I will not attempt to quote all of the applicable Scriptures; however, there are some key foundational principles found in God's Word that must be shared.

1. Abram/Abraham (Genesis 15:12-18) – In this passage of Scripture, God established His covenant with Abram. In verse 12, a deep sleep had fallen upon Abram. In verse 13, the Lord spoke to Abram *while he was asleep.* The covenant that established the Promised Land, which would belong to the descendants of Abram, was made by God while he was asleep.

2. Gideon (Judges 7:13-15) – Gideon overheard a man telling his dream and receiving the interpretation, which confirmed the victory and ultimately gave him the confidence he needed for the battle.

3. Solomon (1 Kings 3:5-15) – The Lord appeared to Solomon in a dream at night according to verse 5. Solomon responded to God's question about giving him what he asked for and requested an understanding mind and a hearing heart to judge the people of God. Solomon desired the ability to discern between good and bad. In short, Solomon's request for wisdom was discussed with God while he was asleep.

4. Peter (2 Peter 1:19-21) – This passage reminds us that prophecy, or prophetic words, are not produced by the will of man. Mankind speaks specifically what is given from God by the Holy Spirit. (Dreams are a delineation of the prophetic gift.)

5. Joel (Joel 2:28) – A familiar passage that emphasizes how the Spirit of God will come upon all flesh, enabling prophecy and dreams, regardless of age.

As you have read, the Bible has much to say about dreams. Hopefully, you have learned that dreams are a valid method of communicating messages to God's people during the night season.

When I am afraid, I put my trust in you.
Psalm 56:3 ESV

CHAPTER TWO

YOUR SLEEP ENVIRONMENT

GOOD SLEEP HYGIENE

As a dreamer, you should pay attention to your sleep hygiene. Sleep hygiene is important. Now, you might be wondering, "What is sleep hygiene?" What does that mean? It means getting enough sleep so that your body is rested. You will need to monitor your sleep environment. You don't want the things you watch on TV or the things you listen to on the radio to interfere with the message that God wants to communicate to you through your dreams.

While some are able to block out any noise while they are sleeping, others cannot. As such, those sounds make their way into your dream and causes you to hear things that were not intended to be a part of that dream. For example, if my husband is playing music in the bedroom while I'm sleeping, I may hear those songs in my dream. Hearing popular or familiar songs might seem nice, but it can impact the reception of dream elements and the overall message being communicated.

Reducing distractions and any interference is key to a good sleep environment. Environment determines what grows and thrives and what does not, so set an atmosphere to hear from God. Cultivate the skill of listening in the dream realm. Do not be quick to assume that what you see is a literal interpretation. Be diligent in the interpretation process, but lean into and trust the Holy Spirit.

Where do dreams come from? There are three primary sources of dreams:

1. The Holy Spirit
2. The demonic realm
3. The soulish realm

God told us in His Word that He would cause an increase in dreams and visions, so it should not come as a surprise that many more people are talking about the dreams they are having.

*And it shall come to pass afterward, that I will pour out my Spirit on **all** flesh your sons and your daughters shall prophesy, your old men shall dream dreams, and your young men shall see visions.*
Joel 2:28 ESV (emphasis added)

So, how do we know that a dream is from God? If you think about the nature of God, messages from Him will not contradict His nature or character, even if it makes you uncomfortable because of the message He needs to speak.

Although God speaks again and again, no one pays attention to what he says. At night when people are asleep, God speaks in dreams and visions. He makes them listen to what he says, and they are frightened at his warnings. God speaks to make them stop their sinning and to save them from becoming proud. He will not let them be destroyed; he saves them from death itself.
Job 33:14-18 GNT

Dreams from God coincide with the voice of God. While it can be authoritative, it is without condemnation and full of mercy. A dream that is from God will agree with Scripture, is life-giving and leads to salvation and/or restoration. In case you're not convinced, there are examples in the Bible of God speaking to people with the evidence of what God said manifesting shortly thereafter.

Solomon loved the LORD, walking in the statutes of David his father, only he sacrificed and made offerings at the high places. At Gibeon the LORD appeared to Solomon in a DREAM by night, and God said, "Ask what I shall give you."

1 Kings 3:3, 5 ESV (emphasis added)

In the same manner that God speaks to people through dreams, the enemy also is the source of some dreams.

While Pilate was sitting in the judgment hall, his wife sent him a message: "Have nothing to do with that innocent man, because in a DREAM last night I suffered much on account of him."

Matthew 27:19 GNT (emphasis added)

You may be one of the people who have read this Scripture but never realized how this was a dream (nightmare) from the enemy. How do we know this was from the enemy? Though Jesus was innocent, if Pilate had listened to his wife and let Him go, it would not have been the will of God, which was ultimately to sacrifice His life on the cross at Calvary. The enemy uses partial truth in his deceit to make it seem legit; but we must always ask about the will of God. That's why it's important to pray and seek God daily, asking Him what message He wants to communicate to you that day.

Dreams from Satan will be accusative or bring fear. It will go against the holy Scriptures or twist the Word. These dreams lead people away from Jesus as Savior and appeal to the flesh. It can also bring death (not just physical death, but death of relationships) and destruction.

Here's another example of the enemy being a source of dreams:

But while his men were sleeping, his enemy came and sowed weeds among the wheat and went away.
Matthew 13:25 ESV

The fact that the deed was done while they were sleeping not only speaks to the work of the enemy that takes place during the night season, but it also speaks to the weeds (in the form of doubts, etc.) that are sown during our dreams while we are sleeping. Spiritual warfare isn't just taking place during waking hours. It takes place during your sleep as well, which is why some of you have had warfare dreams where you are speaking in tongues or casting out demons! More on different types of dreams later.

For though we walk in the flesh, we are not waging war according to the flesh.
2 Corinthians 10:3 ESV

What about soulish dreams? *Soulish dreams* or dreams from your own flesh. These dreams are often self-seeking, promoting your own personal agenda and are not the will of God. It can be filled with insecurity or ways to exalt yourself above others. On some occasions, dreams can be the result of our own soul (mind, will, emotions)—the things that we desire but are not backed by the kingdom of God; however, it can be manipulated by the kingdom of darkness if you don't take those thoughts captive to the obedience of Christ, which is the will of God.

Casting down arguments and every high thing that exalts itself against the knowledge of God, bringing every thought into captivity to the obedience of Christ.
2 Corinthians 10:5 NKJV

Not quite sure what I'm talking about? Perhaps another hint from the Scriptures will help.

The more you worry, the more likely
you are to have bad dreams…
Ecclesiastes 5:3a GNT

God does not want us to worry, but to trust Him. This is another way that our soul can interfere with the dreams we have. When we worry, our minds are not focused on the promises of God. Worrying impacts our sleep routine and ultimately the reception of God speaking to us through our dreams.

INTERFERENCE

It's 1:30 a.m. on the morning of my wedding. I'm wide awake, sitting in an unfamiliar bed. I decided to stow away for the night in a local hotel to avoid some common stressors that make me anxious. This is a very important day for me, so I would rather not experience what physicians have labeled as angioneurotic edema, the swelling of the face with the possibility of hives for no apparent reason. This is a condition that I've struggled with since the age of 20, with no known cause other than stress or emotional anxiety. So, rather than look like Will Smith in "Hitch" on my wedding day, I placed myself on a six-hour rotation of Benadryl with a 24-hour regimen of Claritin.

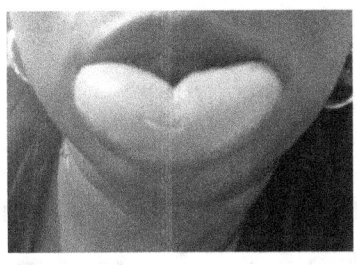

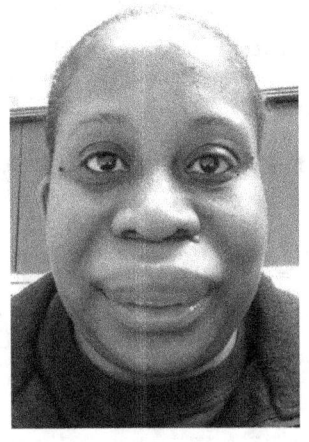

Nine million Americans, four percent of the United States population, cannot sleep without being medicated according to 2021 sleep statistics.[1] Most people deal with some type of worry — worry about debt and finances, worry about ill or elderly loved ones, their own personal health crises, or even the ill-advised choices of their children. Further desensitized by the constant barrage of images from media, there should be no wonder why anxiety and depression are topping the charts of social emotional conditions.

Interference can impact good sleep hygiene because the two sources of interference are biological and audio/visual. The medications you take can have an impact on the dreams you have. Likewise, the things you watch on television and listen to on the radio can impact your dreams. With this in mind, protect your ear gates and your eye gates especially before going to sleep.

My favorite television show used to be *Law and Order: Special Victims Unit (SVU)*. Not only would I watch the show, but I looked forward to marathons. I noticed how after watching a SVU marathon, I would have dreams about sexual violence, kidnapping and other crimes. Immediately, I recognized that it was because of what I watched on TV that my dreams—which had been "normal" up to that point, had taken that turn. This is audio/visual interference.

Audio/visual interference can even happen with the posts that you see on social media right before falling to sleep. Dreams are one of the primary ways that God speaks to me, so I made a personal choice to stop watching certain movies and television shows before bedtime. If it's not watched during the day when I have a chance to counteract the potential impact, I don't watch it at all. Furthermore, I stopped watching television and only watch movies primarily for date nights with the hubby.

We each have our favorite songs and music. I'm not saying don't listen to music, but I am saying listen to the lyrics and what it's encouraging you to do through the confession made when you recite or sing the words. It was amazing to me when I started examining lyrics and realized how perverse they were. Since song lyrics are copywritten, I cannot share any here; however, what are some examples that you can think of as it relates to audio/visual interference? How do you need to protect your eye gates and ear gates?

BIOLOGICAL

Biological interference in dreams simply refers to the medications we take which impacts what we dream about. Whether it is a Tylenol for a headache or some caffeine to stay awake, these things can have an impact on the dreams you have. There are other biological factors that can impact your dreams, too. One of the more popular ones is having to urinate. When you have to urinate while sleeping, many times you will feel the urge to urinate in your dreams. For any children or adults who "wet the bed," or have trouble controlling their bladder, this falls under biological interference as it relates to dreams. You may be having a warning dream, but the message becomes diluted because all of a sudden, you feel the urge to pee.

INSOMNIA

Insomnia is a condition that many people suffer from, whether diagnosed by a medical professional or accepted by themselves as their self-diagnosed "fate." Many times, this starts small and innocently. As children, when you have nightmares, you don't want to have them anymore. You may say an inner vow like, "I never want to dream again!" Such vows can impact your ability to receive messages from God via your dreams later in life. You may also suffer from insomnia because you don't know what to do with the messages you receive when you fall asleep. Too often, the enemy will try to dissuade you from desiring communication through dreams because he knows that there can be warning dreams or calling dreams that pull you out from under his influence. Without the enemy's interruptions and influence, you may actually become the person God desires for you to be, which is a nightmare for the kingdom of darkness.

How then can you combat insomnia from a spiritual perspective? This in no way represents a medical diagnosis or treatment; but as far as your spiritual growth, the following disciplines may be beneficial.

PEACE

I debated with entitling this subheading "anxiety," but I chose "peace" instead. A lot of people who suffer with insomnia also deal with anxiety; however, *peace* is the antidote. For believers in Christ Jesus, He must become our peace. Many have accepted Jesus Christ as Savior, but never learned how to make Him their Lord. To have Jesus as your Lord means you trust Him with every aspect of your life. This includes those people that you have yet to forgive and the situations that you're trying to work out yourself due to your lack of trust in man.

God is not a man, that he should lie; neither the son of man, that he should repent: hath he said, and shall he not do it? or hath he spoken, and shall he not make it good?
Numbers 23:19 KJV

Time for some introspection. What are the situations that you have no trouble praying about? What are the situations that you take to others in your circle—you know, the people you call or text when something happens *before* you take it to God? Let's dig deeper. What are those situations that you tell no one about, not even God? This all reveals a lack of trust and that Jesus is not truly your Lord yet.

It's nothing to be ashamed of; I know this is something that I had to realize and come to grips with myself, which is why I can now write about it. (If it doesn't minister to me first, I'm not about to tell you how to handle it.) Besides, shame and guilt are from the enemy. That's not how God deals with His people. God deals with His people by inquiry.

We find examples of this starting in Genesis when God asked Adam, "Where art thou?" (Genesis 3:9). God also uses conviction by the Holy Spirit, which is designed to bring people closer to Him. You know the difference between condemnation (shame and guilt) and conviction is based on whether you want to hide and be in isolation. Isolation is the enemy's playground. He tries to convince you to believe that no one cares just to get you alone torment you further with his lies. Don't allow yourself to fall into that trap! Find someone who you can be accountable to when you start feeling this way. It could be a mentor, therapist, counselor, friend, minister or another confidant.

During my second year of seminary, I was confronted with my trust issues. While I don't recall the class I was sitting in or the topic of the day, I remember quite distinctly when God told me, "You don't trust me."

"What do you mean, God? I trust you!" My response was typical. That's when He began to show me *myself*. He reminded me of the inner vow I made when my first husband abandoned me. My life changed without my permission, and I vowed that I would *never* trust a man again. That vow somehow included my interactions with God the *Father*.

Although God is not a man but Spirit, my initial view of God was based on what I knew — which is, viewing Him as I would view any other man. God then reminded me of how that vow caused me to become a proud, independent woman who acted like I didn't need to depend on anyone else, including *Him*. If I couldn't get it myself, my mother was my backup before my husband. If that didn't work, I looked for other resources but did not consult God. I could have saved myself some anxiety had I learned early on to seek Him first. That's why we need to read our Bibles daily. It has the answers to questions you haven't even asked.

But seek ye first the kingdom of God, and his righteousness; and all these things shall be added unto you.
Matthew 6:33 KJV

Finally, with regards to anxiety, there is the issue of peace. So many of us have grown up in dysfunctional families and have only known dysfunctional relationships that we don't know what it is like to experience peace. This is another aspect of knowing Jesus Christ as Lord. He desires for us to live in peace in Him, regardless of our personal circumstances. Peace comes when we trust our Lord and Savior in every situation and with every person. His peace eliminates any anxiety, allowing you to get the physical rest your body needs while allowing you to receive those key messages from God during your sleep.

And the peace of God, which surpasses all understanding, will guard your hearts and minds through Christ Jesus.
Philippians 4:7 NKJV

PRAYER

Another aspect to consider as you deal with insomnia is your prayer life. Although I have touched on this briefly in mentioning trusting Jesus as Lord and Savior, it bears repeating in a little more depth. Prayer should not be something you do out of obligation like we did when we were kids before going to bed. Neither should prayer be considered mandatory as a part of some obligation as a member of a church or denomination. Prayer is the ultimate form of communication between the Creator of the universe and His creation. In the same way that you desire to communicate with the people you care about, God wants to communicate with us.

Prayer is not just believers giving a list of requests to God either. That perspective is more akin to Santa Claus or a genie, and neither of which is our Heavenly Father. It is only through prayer that we hear His heart, learn His voice and obey His commands.

My sheep hear My voice, and I know them, and they
follow Me.
John 10:27 NKJV

In the same way that I can recognize my mother's voice and my best friend's voice on the phone without them announcing that it's them, that's the same way that we should recognize God's voice. We should immediately recognize the method God uses to speak to us specifically and the promptings of the Holy Spirit. The promptings of the Holy Spirit are often classified as "something told me," but that's a lesson for another day.

If you do not already talk to God (prayer) on a daily basis, then that should be the first goal for you each day. I recommend starting your day with a conversation with God; but you can make the best choice for you given your schedule. (I know some people work at night, so their days are opposite of mine.) Whatever the case, make it a priority to communicate with God starting once per day and increasing it to where you're talking to God constantly throughout your day.

My final piece of advice regarding prayer is to not compare yourself to anyone else. We are all on a journey and regardless of our physical age, we are starting at different points along the path. Talking to God more than trying to please people will hopefully alleviate these concerns.

MEDITATION

Meditation gets a bad reputation and too many Christians avoid it, thinking that it originated with Eastern religions and philosophies. This couldn't be further from the truth. Meditation is an essential part of the believer's walk as demonstrated in the Old Testament.

*This Book of the law shall not depart from your mouth, but you shall **meditate** in it day and night, that you may observe to do according to all that is written in it. For then you will make your way prosperous, and then you will have good success.*

Joshua 1:8 NKJV (emphasis added)

With Christian meditation, we don't need to sit with our legs like pretzels nor do we need to chant or have special music playing. It is wise to set an atmosphere of worship any time that you are seeking the presence of the Lord, though the type of worship music is a personal preference. What does it mean to "set an atmosphere"? Think of your five senses and how those can be prepped for worship.

You may play instrumental worship songs, which is an auditory experience. You may also have natural light coming in the room, which is a visual experience. You can also begin to recite your favorite Scriptures or Biblical affirmations, which creates a verbal experience. Your hearing is being engaged from the music playing and the words being spoken. Finally, is the sense of smell. Some people are able to smell the "sweet, smelling aroma" that comes with the presence of God; but on the opposite end, you don't want the smell of your favorite dish in the kitchen distracting you to rush this precious time with the Lord.

The goal of meditation is to focus our thoughts on God, to reflect on His Word and to seek His face — not only for what decisions to make, but to listen for what He desires to communicate to *you* — His child, His servant in the earth realm, and His heir.

And if children, then heirs — heirs of God and joint heirs with Christ, if indeed we suffer with Him, that we may also be glorified together.
Romans 8:17 NKJV

Take My yoke upon you and learn from Me,
for I am gentle and lowly in heart,
and you will find rest for your souls.
Matthew 11:29 ESV

CHAPTER THREE

DREAMS

Darkness was everywhere.

I had the feeling in the pit of my stomach like I was barreling over the edge of a steep roller coaster. Being in this space seemed as if I was a part of the darkness or completed enveloped by it. I only remember seeing streaks of silver and then feeling as if a simple touch would wreak eternal havoc. Something as simple as bending my finger exposed thousands of intricacies that I did not understand, and it scared me. I would fight to wake up from this recurring dream that lasted from age six until at least 16.

Did you have recurring dreams as a child? Have you ever wondered what your dreams mean? Do your dreams hold valuable messages that you're missing? Dreams are one of the ways in which God communicates with the earth realm. According to James W. Goll, "A dream is a series of thoughts, images or emotions that appear in our minds during sleep."[2] A dream is comprised of revelations, or something that is being revealed.

My greatest passion has always been teaching. The information shared within this book is to teach you about the things that have puzzled you for too long. Training is needed in order to be a good steward over your dreams. Activation is the final step to you not only receiving the revelations of your dreams, but using them to manifest the will of God in the earth realm. This book was birthed from the dream interpretation workshops held by Visions International Ministry, where I serve as senior pastor.

At Visions International, our goal is to teach, train and activate those called to leadership to heal from trauma and experience victory over darkness so they can walk in their divine destiny. God has already done all of the things that He intended to do. The rest is up to us—His ambassadors in the earth. Let's build the skills necessary to make that happen.

Ninety percent of the dreams you have, at least initially, are personal and not meant to be shared publicly. Keeping a dream journal helps you document your dreams. This is critical for being a good steward over your dream anointing. Writing down your dreams will also help you to receive the messages with clarity, which is key for discovering the source of each dream, who the dreams are for, the type(s) of dreams you have and what to do with the revelation received in your dreams. There are specific questions that I will share later in this book so you can better understand the message after each dream.

In the first year that Belshazzar was king of Babylonia, I had a dream and saw a vision in the night. I wrote the dream down, and this is the record of what I saw that night...
Daniel 7:1-2 GNT

SOURCES OF DREAMS

When you wake up from a dream, the first question to ask yourself is the source of the dream. Clues to this would be the emotions you feel when you wake up: Are you scared? Do you feel a sense of peace? Are you recalling scenes from a television show or movie you watched? These are all clues to the source of the dream. The source can be one of three things: either it's from God through the Holy

Spirit; it's from Satan through demonic spirits, or the source is your human soul.

Dreams from God give information, direction or reveal some part of God's plan. Dreams from the enemy come to cause fear or to have you come into agreement with the enemy's plan by providing legal access through violating God's laws. When the source is your own soul, this includes varying types of interference that was discussed in chapter two.

For the Lord GOD does NOTHING without revealing His secret to His servants the prophets.
Amos 3:7 ESV (emphasis added)

Up to 80% of your dreams are going to have a personal message for you, but how will you know? Many times in dreams, you are involved in the action. These are dreams that are for you or impact you in some way. Other dreams have you watching the action. You are either looking at actions taking place through a window or from a different position where you are not involved, but the dream is playing out before you like a movie on a screen. These are definitely dreams that could have a message for others. If the dream is in that ten percent and is not personally about you, here are the questions to ask yourself:

- Is this a dream to tell someone else? Once you wake up, you may get a burden (can't shake the feeling or let it go) that you need to communicate with the person in the dream. Pray first, and then proceed as the Holy Spirit leads. Be sure not to give into the desire to share with others as gossip. That is not operating in the Spirit of God. If it is to tell, you tell that person specifically and not others. No "Guess what I dreamed about Sister Cornbread last night?" Please and thank you.

- Is this dream to intercede about in prayer? Usually this dream disturbs you to some degree. You may see an accident, illness or some other calamity. These are definitely dreams to intercede or immediately pray about so it does not come to pass. We have that ability as believers. In the same way that God chose to communicate the dream to you, He needs someone in the earth realm to combat the intended course in the spirit realm before it happens in the earth realm.

- Is this a dream to record and save for a different time? All dreams should be recorded with a date. If you are not prompted to immediate action, as in calling the person or praying, then it is to record and review later. You can set your own pace to review dreams, whether it is monthly, quarterly or yearly. This is all a part of being a good steward over our dreams.

The best practice is to record the dream in your dream journal, and then ask these questions during your prayer time with God before you ever mention the dream to someone else.

Let's start with an understanding that dreams and visions are biblical. One third of the Bible includes dreams and visions. Many things took place while people in the Bible were asleep. A vision is not your imagination or wishful thinking. It is a supernatural depiction of a scene that you see with your physical eyes playing out while your eyes are open. It is often superimposed in the physical space that you are occupying.

A dream is referred to as a "vision of the night" (Job 33:15). You are asleep and your eyes are closed, but you are watching scenes play out in your "mind's eye." Dreams and visions are similar, but they're not the same primarily because dreams can be influenced by biological means or other types of interference. We have excellent examples of dreams with Solomon and Gideon.

Did you know that when Solomon was granted wisdom, it was because God appeared to him in his dream? That's what we learned in 1 Kings 3:3-5. Yes, it was the result of a dream from God, which came after Solomon made a choice to no longer offer sacrifices at the wrong altar, but made a worthy sacrifice to the Lord to show there had been a change. We see here that we can love the Lord, walk in His statutes and yet still do things that are displeasing to God like sacrificing to other gods. When we discover the error of our ways and repent, that's when the blessing comes. This all can be revealed in dreams.

Gideon had a good lesson that was the result of a dream, as well. The people of God did evil in the sight of the Lord, and as a result, they were delivered into the hand of the Midianites. This lasted for seven years, destroying everything and leaving God's people impoverished. God reminded them who He is and not to fear. God sent an angel to speak to Gideon to let him know that God was with him. That wasn't enough to convince Gideon that he was the one for this task, so God allowed Gideon to overhear the telling and interpretation of the opposing soldier's dream.

And when Gideon had come, there was a man telling a dream to his companion. He said, "I have had a dream: To my surprise, a loaf of barley bread tumbled into the camp of Midian; it came to a tent and struck it so that it fell and overturned, and the tent collapsed." Then his companion answered and said, "This is nothing else but the sword of Gideon the son of Joash, a man of Israel! Into his hand God has delivered Midian and the whole camp." And so it was, when Gideon heard the telling of the dream and its interpretation, that he worshipped. He returned to the camp of Israel, and said, "Arise, for the LORD has delivered the camp of Midian into your hand."

Judges 7:13-15 NKJV

Just as here with Gideon, God allowed a dream to provide the assurance of victory that was needed because the result was already secured in the spirit realm. Dream interpretation is beyond just the symbols and their meanings, but also understanding that the dream realm is a representation of the spiritual realm. The spiritual realm is where the future is determined, even before it manifests in the physical or earth realm. This is a foundational understanding that's needed before we discuss dream symbols.

20 TYPES OF DREAMS

The final piece for this work is to discuss the types of dreams. In my experience, there are at least twenty different types of dreams. Knowing the types of dreams that God uses, as He is speaking to His people, should help you to capture messages you may have missed previously.

1. Warning Dreams – These dreams warn of an impending danger or situation that you must be cautious about. These are always absolute and not just for the sake of knowledge. You can rebuke these dreams or intercede for the person before the calamity takes place.

In the second year of the reign of Nebuchadnezzar, Nebuchadnezzar had dreams; his spirit was troubled, and his sleep left him...Then the mystery was revealed to Daniel in a vision of the night. Then Daniel blessed the God of heaven...A great God has made known to the king what shall be after this. The dream is certain and its interpretation sure.
Daniel 2: 1, 19, 45b ESV

2. Direction Dreams – Oftentimes, we ask God for direction. We want to know which way to go. Direction dreams provide that answer.

Now when they had departed, behold, an angel of the Lord appeared to Joseph in a DREAM and said, "Rise, take the child and his mother, and flee to Egypt, and remain there until I tell you, for Herod is about to search for the child, to destroy him."
Matthew 2:13 ESV (emphasis added)

3. Confirmation Dreams – Perhaps you have already received an answer to prayer, but you want to be certain that it's God and not another voice or even self. A confirmation dream lets you know with certainty that the message is from God.

4. Calling/Destiny Dreams – If you are a dreamer, God will often show you a snapshot of what is to come in your future. These are destiny dreams that confirm the calling on your life.

5. Warfare Dreams – Spiritual warfare is constantly taking place. With warfare dreams, God selects the person that He knows will pray warfare prayers for the desired outcome.

6. Recurring Dreams – A recurring dream is a vital message that God wants you to receive a specific message. The message is so important that He puts it on repeat.

7. Foresight Dreams – Foresight dreams give you knowledge about a future event. God allows you to see something as insight into a situation.

8. Deliverance Dreams – Yes, you can receive deliverance in your dream. Also, you can be prepared to minister deliverance in your dream. Deliverance dreams show a demon being cast out or you are engaging in deliverance to assist someone else to receive their freedom from bondage. Dreams

like this can help to prepare you for what is to come in reality.

9. Healing Dreams – Healing can happen physically, emotionally, psychologically and mentally. It can take place while you are awake or while you are asleep. You can be in a hospital setting or at home; but when you awaken, you sense that healing has actually taken place.

10. Purging Dreams – There are areas in our lives where a particular "room" needs to be cleaned out. It could be based on a relationship or the role you play. Purging dreams evict things that should not be present and things that are not beneficial for God's will in your life.

11. Instruction Dreams – These dreams are similar to direction dreams; however, instruction dreams tell you the next steps. You discover not just which way

to go, but what to do now that you know which way to go.

12. Revelation of God Dreams – These dreams are primarily for those who are just getting to know God. These are for people who are not necessarily believers or committed to the faith. They desire to know if God is real, so He shows up in their dream(s) to show an aspect of His character.

13. Dreams of Comfort – Comfort is a basic human need. These dreams often happen after a loss of some kind. God can provide comfort in many ways; but for the dreamer, this soothes the heart and mind, allowing you to feel how much the Father loves you.

14. Dreams of Correction – When we step outside the will of God, dreams of correction are one way for Him to get your attention. These dreams let you know that you need to take immediate steps of

correction. Do not delay when you receive this type of dream.

15. Dreams of Impartation – Impartation is primarily around gifts. If God desires you to walk in a new gifting or anointing, that impartation can happen in a dream. You may see yourself singing on stage or speaking from a podium. God is imparting a new level in you to accomplish His will.

16. Dreams of Intercession – Just as God can awaken you to pray for someone in the middle of the night, He can also impress upon you in your sleep to intercede for someone. It could be based on what you see happening in the dream, based on the person that you see or hear their name in the dream. Dreams of intercession should be taken seriously, as it could be life or death.

17. Word of Knowledge Dreams – If you have been praying about an area or situation, a word of

knowledge can come in your dream while you are asleep. A word of knowledge is a clue to a puzzle that is yet to take place. Futuristic in nature, this key can unlock doors for you or others.

18. Dreams of Creativity – God is the Creator and we are creative people. Many ideas, inventions and projects can be birthed in the dream realm. The question becomes what will you do with the creative thought once you have it.

19. Dreams of Exhortation – Exhortation is to bring a message of urgency. It is a method of communication that causes people to act.

20. Cleansing Dreams – Cleansing dreams do exactly what it states. They cleanse you – whether it is a soul cleansing to remove residue of past trauma or painful memories; or whether it is a follow-up to cleanse prior habits and behaviors that do not support where you are going in Christ.

And the peace of God, which surpasses all understanding, will guard your hearts and your minds in Christ Jesus.
Philippians 4:7 ESV

CHAPTER FOUR

NIGHTMARES

Where do nightmares come from? If you refer back to the three sources of dreams, nightmares come from the demonic realm, specifically the kingdom of darkness. Nightmares are designed to illicit fear to provide an open door for legal access into the life of the dreamer. Nightmares are common in children and new believers, commonly referred to as "babes in Christ." Most times, when you have nightmares, you want them to stop. Some people, even as a child, will make an inner vow regarding dreams that cuts off this revelation from not just the demonic realm, but also from God. The enemy does not want you to walk in revelation from God through your dreams.

Thou shalt not be afraid for the terror by night; nor for
the arrow that flieth by day;
Psalm 91:5 KJV

The night stalker demon learns critical skills for serious hits against those with the prophetic anointing to dream. Night stalkers watch you to determine your weakness and uses it against you. There are three groups of night stalkers: lurkers, haunters and clingers. Lurkers watch you in private to learn when it is the best time to attack. Haunters torment their victims to cause fright and trauma. Clingers stick with you wherever you go, which is why 1 Peter 5:8 warns us to be sober and vigilant.

Nightmares typically come in three ways: dark dreams, dreams of fear or panic, and dreams of deception. Dark dreams are dreams that make you feel somber or depressed. It brings fear and insecurity. These dreams present with a black, grey or muted background, and "something feels wrong or off." Darkness is the cover by which demonic spirits attack. Legal rights to torment could come from prayerlessness, masturbation, anger, greed, pornography, drunkenness or other "open doors" or points of access.

Yea, though I walk through the valley of the shadow of death, I will fear no evil; For You are with me; Your rod and Your staff, they comfort me.
Psalm 23:4 NKJV

Most childhood dreams fall into the category of fear or panic. We must rebuke these dreams and invite the Holy Spirit in. You can invite the Holy

Spirit in by saying the words "Holy Spirit, you are welcome in my home, my life and in my mind." You can also invite the Holy Spirit in the same way you would invite a guest to come visit. It can be a part of your daily prayers, especially before falling asleep. If these dreams continue, you must assess your sleep environment. Check your environment for cursed items and ask the Lord to expose the root so that repentance and healing can take place. Cursed items include items like those connected to idol worship, demonic games, jewelry connected to idols, deities or demonic spirits to name a few. It is okay to teach children how to rebuke the devil, to speak the Word of God and focus on Jesus. Children listen daily to voices on the television, in movies, in video content on streaming services, video games and the Internet. Something is always speaking to them; so if we fail to teach them about God, how can we expect them to desire Him when they are older?

The final type of nightmares are dreams of deception. This can happen at any age and is not limited to childhood. Dreams of deception are designed to get us to turn away from the truth in God's Word in order to gain information (to use against you), gain agreement, forge a demonic covenant, sacrifice to an evil altar or to "infect you." Be careful about signing any documents in dreams, answering personal questions in dreams, being stuck with a needle, getting bit by an animal or something as "innocent" as a hug, kiss, eating or drinking in a dream.

Having sex in a dream is another way that covenants are formed since sex is a covenantal act. Even if it is your spouse, this is likely a masquerading spirit pretending to be your spouse in order to gain that covenant or agreement. The most common spirits you unknowingly come into agreement with are the spirits of poverty and/or sickness. No one is allowed to legally "build" without a permit. The enemy needs a permit—your permission—to build any fortress or stronghold, which is a war in your mind, to keep you in a sin cycle.

Lest Satan should take advantage of us;
for we are not ignorant of his devices.
2 Corinthians 2:11 NKJV

DREAMS ABOUT THE DECEASED

I saved dreaming of deceased relatives for this chapter—not to offend, but to deal with the evil that it represents for what it is. Many people struggle after losing a loved one and desire to hear from them again to know they are "okay." This is what is referred to as necromancy, which is the practice of communicating with the dead, especially to know what to do or predict the future. The enemy exploits this through familiar spirits.

And when they say to you, "Inquire of the mediums and the necromancers who chirp and mutter," should not a people inquire of their God? Should they inquire of the dead on behalf of the living?
Isaiah 8:19 ESV

Familiar spirits often sound like or act like a deceased loved one. They show up in your dreams so you are deceived into hugging or kissing them based on your emotional state of grief. That kiss, hug or even a handshake becomes a point of agreement—not with your loved one, but with a demon providing legal access for the kingdom of darkness in your life. Familiar spirits represent an ancestral spirit that is seeking to maintain a family covenant that is often tied to an evil altar. In the same way that believers give and receive sacrifices for God, the kingdom of darkness mimics these sacrifices and "blessings," but at an evil altar.

God wants us to seek Him alone. As believers in Christ Jesus, regardless how much you miss that person, there is no coming back once their physical body dies (See the story of the rich man and Lazarus in Luke 16:19-31). You may miss them, but that's not your relative you are communicating with in your dreams. If you rebuke that interaction, the person you thought was a relative will often be exposed as the demon they are. When you see the face of that demon spirit or see their presence become distorted, it will be easier to command them to leave and not come back in Jesus' name.

A masquerading spirit represents a demonic spirit in disguise. It is designed to earn your trust by "masquerading" as something you are comfortable with or trust. The goal is to gain an agreement or initiate a covenant. Both familiar spirits and masquerading spirits attempt to take advantage of your emotional state after a loss. Don't be fooled and do not sin against God by communicating in any manner with the dead.

When you believe the lie, you empower the liar. Do not believe the lies of the enemy, particularly when it comes to engaging with a deceased loved one, a spouse, previous lover, current lover or secret crush in your dreams. A simple way to respond to dreams where you are unsure if its God or the devil, just say "God, if this dream is from you, I receive it; but if not, I reject it now in Jesus' name."

THE LAW OF THE ALTAR – EXODUS 20:24B GNT
"…In every place that I set aside for you to worship me, I will come to you and bless you."

THE LAW OF MANIFESTATION – JEREMIAH 29:10 ESV
"For thus says the LORD: When seventy years are completed for Babylon, I will visit you, and I will fulfill to you my promise and bring you back to this place."

Manifestation happens when there is AGREEMENT between the spirit realm and the physical realm.

Curses cannot hurt you unless you deserve them.
Proverbs 26:2a GNT

CLOSING OPEN DOORS

In order to close open doors, you must first recognize them. Doors are opened in your life due to inherited demons, those things based down in your family that are "traditions" you've never questioned, which violated God's spiritual laws. This could be something as simple as having sexual relations in your dreams with a crush or unknown person. Seems harmless and fulfills a desire, but falls in the realm of demonic deception. You must reject these dreams and close that door.

Open doors can also come as a result of a dysfunctional home with rejection, rebellion, divorce, abuse or trauma. If you are constantly fighting in your dreams, the enemy is likely trying to maintain this stronghold in your life. Strongholds start with how we mentally process a situation. If you have a dream where you are fighting someone you already don't like, more than likely, you will not rebuke that dream. It feels good to the flesh, but goes against who you are as a believer in Christ Jesus.

Open doors could also be found in your daily habits like the type of movies you watch, particularly horror movies, which invite a spirit of fear; or rated R movies that often have sex scenes and/or nudity which promotes sexual immorality. The more you think about how the enemy has gained access to your life, the easier it will become to recognize those open doors and close them.

Why is it important to close those doors? Until those doors of access are closed to the enemy, the dreams you have will not all be messages from God. It's like cleaning your filter. By processing out the dreams from the enemy or dreams based on your selfish, fleshly desires, you increase the godly dreams that have a direct impact on what God desires to say to you.

CLEANSING YOUR HOME

Cleansing—not cleaning, your home is just as important as closing those open doors. Cleaning your house is basic maintenance to remove any physical impurities and harmful substances. Cleansing your home does the same, but spiritually. As long as the enemy has something that belongs to him in your home, he has access. Things that belong to the enemy include accursed items. Accursed items are things that invite demonic activity because of the symbolic meaning or the fact that it was dedicated to a demonic spirit.

Accursed items can include anything related to zodiac signs; any occultic items, games or paraphernalia used in occultic activities such as a Ouija board, or bracelets, charms, dreamcatchers, books, etc. It could even be something given to you by someone who desires to "look" into your life or control your behaviors through witchcraft practices.

PRAYERS OF PROTECTION

Below is a prayer of protection that can be prayed before bed to block fear from creeping in as you are asleep. This works in combination with your belief system and active participation in removing any items that can cause sleep disturbances or nightmares, as mentioned earlier. You would also do good to familiarize yourself with spiritual weapons. Learning how to use each of the spiritual weapons listed below will work to your benefit as you grow in faith.

- Prayer
- Worship
- The Holy Scriptures
- Repentance
- The whole armor of God (Ephesians 6:11-18)
- The name of Jesus
- The blood of Jesus

Heavenly Father,

I believe the Scripture found in Proverbs 3:24 that says when I lay down, I will not be afraid. When I lie down, my sleep will be sweet. My trust and rest are in You, in Jesus' name. Amen.

For God gave us a spirit not of fear
but of power and love and self-control.
2 Timothy 1:7 ESV

CHAPTER FIVE

WHAT IT ALL MEANS

This book provided some of the information needed to initiate an understanding of the dream realm. The key to interpretation is to remember that all dreams need interpretation, and interpretation belongs to God. Ask the Holy Spirit for insight in understanding your dreams. God will use familiar terms and symbols that you know, so personal context and culture play a factor in interpretation.

Some dreams will only be understood at a future time, so be sure to record the date as you are documenting your dreams in a dream journal. The date is important because it could be key to recognizing an established pattern. There is no harm in asking lots of questions to get a better understanding. God can handle any questions you may have.

Knowing this first of all, that no prophecy of Scripture comes from someone's own interpretation. For no prophecy was ever produced by the will of man, but men spoke from God as they were carried along by the Holy Spirit.

2 Peter 1:20-21 ESV

DREAM SYMBOLS

With the record of your dreams, you can begin to look for patterns and symbols that can lead to a better understanding of how God speaks to you. You should always rely on the Holy Spirit for the interpretation of the dream for we cannot do the work of the Lord without Him.

There are eight categories of symbols in Scripture: objects, creatures (animals), actions, numbers, names, colors, directions and places. Each of these categories will be explored in more detail; but before we do, here are some additional questions to ask about your dream(s):

- What is the main action in the dream? What are you doing? Are you a participant in the dream? Are you involved in the action or are you watching the action like a scene playing out in front of you?
- What is the main emotion in the dream? We already discussed the main emotion you feel when you wake up; but how are you feeling while in the dream?

The proper response to any dream is prayer. A simple prayer that you can say when you wake up is:

Heavenly Father, if this dream is from you, I receive it as Your will. If it is not, I cancel it now and rebuke it in Jesus' name. Amen.

For those who are a bit more mature with an understanding of the spiritual warfare that takes place in dreams, here is a much more specific prayer to repeat after you wake up from a dream:

Heavenly Father, I renounce and come against any agreement or covenant with the powers of darkness achieved in my dream, knowingly or unknowingly. I cancel any spirit that opposes the Holy Spirit and Your will for my life. Lord, I ask that You sever all spiritual restrictions and limitations brought about by witchcraft and the occult. Lord, destroy any demonic altars that are controlling my life. I repent for going against Your Word and Your laws in Jesus' name. Amen.

During prayer, you can clarify what you believe to be the message you have received in your dreams. Context is also key. A symbol can mean one thing to you, but something completely different to someone else. For example, if you are a pet owner, a dog may be a friendly symbol to you; however, if another person was bit by a dog as a child and is terrified of dogs, that could be a very different interpretation.

POPULAR DREAM SYMBOLS

A house – If you dream of a house, particularly a house that you used to live in, it speaks of your life during that time frame. If you dream of a house that you do not recognize, it speaks of confusion. Since God is not the author of confusion, you need to cancel the assignment of that dream and break any agreement made in the dream, whether known or unknown.

A car – Dreams of being in a car usually speak to personal ministry. Likewise, other modes of transportation can have similar meanings. For example, a bus can speak to the size of the ministry; whereas, an airplane can refer to a worldwide ministry. You will also want to note if you are driving the car. If not, who is the person driving? Where are you in the car — are you in the passenger seat? The backseat? Is the car moving forward or is it going backwards? Again, the direction the vehicle is moving in adds more details to the interpretation, so it's important to remember and jot down. Does the car have any damage? Does it have a flat tire? Are other people in the car with you? These details can significantly alter the meaning of the dream.

A school – Dreaming of being in school, unless you are actually enrolled in the school you see in your dreams, speaks of delay. Pay attention to see if you are going up or down the stairs at school. Going downstairs is one of those symbolic actions that speaks of going backwards, another sign of delay. This is another one of those dreams that you want to cancel when you wake up. An example of the prayer to declare immediately upon waking up is:

Jesus Christ is my Lord and Savior. Him and Him only will I serve. I cancel all demonic agreements and break every demonic covenant. I destroy every evil altar and the plan of the enemy in my life, in the name of my Lord and Savior, Jesus Christ, AMEN.

OTHER SYMBOLIC ACTIONS

Going upstairs in a dream could have a positive meaning of being elevated or getting a promotion. Here's another friendly reminder that context is key. Pay attention to the other details, writing as much detail down as possible as soon as you wake up so you can seek a proper interpretation.

Being naked in a dream is another common occurrence. Ask yourself where you were when you were naked. Was anyone else present with you? Were you embarrassed or were you walking around as if everything was normal? Each of these changes the possible interpretation.

Do you recall ever dreaming of your teeth falling out? Losing teeth in a dream, outside of children who are at the age of losing their baby teeth, typically shows a lack of wisdom. If you have missing teeth, it represents the fear of getting older, decay or a fast lifestyle.

Additional popular dream symbols include windows, which represent a future time; and doors, which represents opportunity. With doors, there are additional questions to keep in mind:

- Is the door closed? This could speak of a blocked opportunity.
- Is the door open? This could speak of a new opportunity.
- Are multiple doors locked? This could speak of lack of access.
- Is a cat or dog blocking the door? This could mean there is a spiritual hindrance; the animal will let you know what type of hindrance it is so that you can direct your prayers accordingly.

Storms are another popular dream symbol which typically represent your emotions. If you see a tornado in your dream, you may be experiencing emotional distress or there is a fast-approaching emotional concern. If it is a hurricane, it represents spiritual distress or a fast-approaching spiritual concern. Tornadoes start on land, while hurricanes initiate on the water.

Babies are so cute and adorable, so you would think that they mean something nice in a dream, right? This is not always the case. Again, context is key. If you are of child-bearing age, a baby could have a very different meaning than someone who is menopausal. Personal context and relevance should be remembered.

If you are pregnant in a dream, it could mean that God is birthing something new in you. If you are being passed a baby in your dream, the baby could represent a burden or having someone dependent on you. Pay attention to the person passing you the baby. Do you recognize the person or not? Is the person's face hidden or veiled? Veiled or hidden faces could symbolize something that is hidden or being kept from you. Pay attention!

Eating in a dream is common—until you realize that your spirit man has no need of physical food. So why would you be eating in a dream? The enemy uses things that seem normal to us in waking life to get us to come into agreement unknowingly in the dream realm.

Do I imply, then, that an idol or the food offered to it really amounts to anything? No! What I am saying is that what is sacrificed on pagan altars is offered to demons, not to God. And I do not want you to be partners with demons.

1 Corinthians 10:19-20 GNT

Paul is letting us know that eating can have grave consequences. This symbolism is true in our dreams, as well. When you eat at their feasts, you form a fellowship (agreement) with demonic spirits. Beware of eating in your dreams! You could be forming an agreement without realizing it.

In the dream realm, your spirit man is awake, though your physical body is asleep. Anything you put inside of you to eat in a dream is a pollutant. You are polluting your spirit man! If someone gives you something to eat in a dream, you are coming into agreement with them and what they represent. We just learned from the Apostle Paul that demonic spirits operate in this manner in the dream/spirit realm. The enemy causes us to sin against God and break His rules/principles in this manner, then accuses us of the very thing we did unknowingly. Remember, the enemy is the accuser of the brethren, even if he sets up the scenario for him to accuse us in the courtroom of heaven.

TEN DREAM SYMBOL CATEGORIES

Dreams provide additional understanding in an area; however, you must consider the context, the content, the connection(s) and seeking God to draw a conclusion, which is the proper interpretation.

Symbolic Colors

If the scene in your dream appears dark, this could indicate a demonic presence or that you are spiritually unaware in this situation. Pay attention to it and make note in your dream journal of the colors you see, as well as how the sky looks or makes you feel.

- Black – sin, death, mystery or witchcraft
- Blue – heaven, revelation or the Holy Spirit
- Red – blood, sacrifice, power or war
- White – purity, light, righteousness or a religious spirit

- Green – life, prosperity, intercession or jealousy
- Gold – glory or holiness
- Silver – redemption, grace or legalism
- Brown – compassion, humility or compromise
- Pink – love, being childlike or childish
- Orange – perseverance or stubbornness
- Purple – royalty or authority
- Yellow – joy or hope

Numbers In Dreams

Numbers are important to God and have similar meanings in the Bible as they do in dreams. Most numbers in dreams are literal, unless there is some personal relevance or significance. That's why context is key and cannot be overemphasized.

Here are a few common numbers and their meanings:
- One (1) – beginning, source or unity
- Two (2) – witness, testimony or union
- Three (3) – restoration or triune God
- Four (4) – God's creative works

- Five (5) – grace or redemption
- Six (6) – man or beast
- Seven (7) – perfection or completion
- Eight (8) – new beginnings
- Nine (9) – judgment, harvest or finality
- Ten (10) – wilderness, journey or law
- Eleven (11) - transition
- Twelve (12) – government or apostolic fullness
- Thirteen (13) – rebellion, backsliding or apostasy
- Fourteen (14) – double anointing
- Fifteen (15) – mercy or reprieve
- Sixteen (16) – love or established beginnings
- Seventeen (17) – victory or immaturity
- Eighteen (18) – bondage or oppression
- Forty (40) – testing or trial
- One hundred eleven (111)– my beloved son
- Eight hundred eighty-eight (888) – resurrection
- Ten thousand (10,000) - maturity

Symbolic Places

- Childhood home – represents your earlier life

- Current home – represents your present life/circumstances
- School – while this can represent a place of teaching and learning, it can also represent a spirit of delay, particularly if you are not a current student. If you are considering going back to school, it can be a confirmation.
- Church – represents your faith and/or can indicate fellowship
- Airport – represents a transition, preparation, spiritual refueling or awaiting destiny
- Hotel – represents a temporary place
- Hospital – represents healing or rebuilding
- Elevator – represents entering the spirit realm
- Sports Arena – represents moving in faith or spiritual warfare in a public space

Symbolic People

- Drug Dealer – dependence; temper; manipulation
- Plumber – anointed ministry connecting others together

- Police Officer – spiritual authority; protection; critical spirit
- Race Car Driver – competitive spirit
- Teacher – revelation; the Holy Spirit; a fleshly or false teacher

Symbolic Vehicles

- Airplane – new heights; high profile ministry; travel
- Wheelchair – infirmity; not walking by faith
- Bus – large ministry; vehicle to destiny
- Double-decker bus – prophetic/teaching ministry
- Van – business outlook; delivery/deliverer
- Train – ministry with clout; ministry with an agenda

Symbolic Actions in Dreams

- Falling – loss of control
- Running – a race of faith; contending for your faith

- Walking upstairs – elevation or growth
- Walking downstairs – demotion or delay
- Being chased – being threatened or pursued by a spiritual or physical enemy; call to prayer
- Crossing the street – making a choice/decision; could represent deliverance
- Being stuck – warning of danger; could represent a stronghold
- Being in an alley – having something to hide or having an unprepared heart
- Bitten by an animal - betrayal
- Going in circles – wandering; uncertainty; confusion
- Having sex – union or agreement; lust
- Signing documents – sealed agreement; ownership

Symbolic Animals

- Bear – strength, judgment
- Polar Bear – religious spirit
- Beaver – busy, clever, diligent
- Bull – persecution, spiritual warfare, accusation, opposition

- Cat – unclean spirit, sneaky, deception, untrainable
- Cheetah – danger, fast predator
- Chicken – cowardice or fear
- Crab – not easy to approach, standoffish
- Crow/Raven – confusion, envy/strife, hateful
- Cow – prosperity
- Deer – swift, agile
- Dinosaur – ancient stronghold, generational curse,
- past danger
- Dog – loyalty, protection or betrayal
- Dove – Holy Spirit
- Eagle – prophetic calling
- Elephant – great impact, not easily offended, powerful
- Fish – the souls of mankind
- Fox – sly or scheming individual
- Frog – spirit of lust
- Goat – lack of discernment
- Horse – military, power
- Monkey – mischief or addition
- Owl – monitoring spirit(s)
- Panther (black) – high-level witchcraft

- Pig – ignorance, selfish, gluttonous
- Rabbit – fast growth or increase
- Sheep – innocent, vulnerable, sacrifice, people of God
- Snake – accusation, unforgiveness, lying
- Spiders – witchcraft, occult
- Turtle/Tortoise – slow change
- Whale – spiritual impact
- Wolf – false ministries and false teachers

Symbolic Insects

- Bee – strong demonic attack
- Butterfly – freedom, transformation
- Flies – evil spirits, occultic, dead things
- Grasshopper – destruction
- Roach – infestation, hidden sin
- Scorpion – evil spirits and evil men
- Spiders – witchcraft, occult
- Spider web – the place of demonic attack, ensnarement

Symbolic Clothing

- Being naked (no clothes) – feeling exposed or vulnerable
- Cardigan/gown – human cover-up

Symbolic Directions

- East – birth, first, beginning
- West – end, grace, death, last
- North – spiritual judgment, heaven, spiritual warfare
- South – sin, world, temptation, flesh, corruption
- Right – authority, power, strength of man, the power of God revealed through man, salvation, wisdom
- Left – justice, sinister or foolishness

These dream symbols are by no means an exhaustive list. This is meant to provide a snapshot of popular dream symbols so that you can start building your proficiency of understanding your own dreams, in consultation with God through His

Holy Spirit. Never rely solely on a dream book or dream symbols to figure out the messages from God. Seek His face and He will provide you with exactly what He needs you to know and how to respond.

COUNTERFEIT INTERPRETATIONS

Counterfeit interpretations are simply interpretations of godly communication that does not come from God. The interpretation can come from the soul (mind, will, emotions) of the person or from the kingdom of darkness. A lot of people believe they can interpret dreams, but you must ask their source. Where are they getting their information? Is it based on tradition, or what other relatives have said? Is it from Google? Is it from a website that is ran by a different belief system other than Christianity? Is the source someone who dabbles in magic, astrology or the dark arts? These are some examples of counterfeit interpretations. Keep in mind that God has a plan for your life, but so does Satan. Each one's sources will push you closer to their destiny for your life. Will you choose God or Satan?

There is nothing wrong with seeking to interpret your own dreams. That's what the content in this book is empowering you to do with the help of the Holy Spirit. The key is to learn the Word of God since His Word will never contradict a message God is giving you in a dream. It is also key to be consistent in prayer. You should not seek to do the work of God without Him. Dreams can help you to hear God personally.

It is also acceptable to seek the support of a dream analyst until you are able to interpret on your own. You may be wondering what the difference is between a dream interpreter and a dream analyst. Dream interpretation is a gift, but also an art that can be learned. Training and practice allows you to learn dream interpretation; however, a dream analyst analyzes the dream symbols, using the gift of dream interpretation while seeking revelation by the Holy Spirit to deliver the intended message.

Exploring the Dream Mystery

There are times when we may have a conflicting message from a dream and not know what to do.

Whenever there is a conflict between symbols or meanings, review the initial dream journal entry to view it in the intended context. Be aware of any personal meanings of the symbols for the person who dreamed that dream. You will also want to be attentive to cultural meanings around specific objects, celebrations or traditions. This can vary between communities. Ask questions about what items are used for or what they are made of to gain deeper understanding which can lead to the proper interpretation.

When a dream "shifts" or it seems as if the dreamer "hopped" from one dream to another, the two dreams can be related. Sometimes, the first dream and its symbolism can present a question and the second or subsequent dream presents a solution. Those who have multiple dreams in one night without being awakened may be familiar with this phenomenon. This is just one possibility that should be remembered as you grow in your knowledge of dream interpretation.

Perhaps you've read up until this point and you're aware of the fact that most of the time, you don't even remember your dreams. Some people don't believe that they have dreams, but the truth is that many just do not remember. Avoid saying things like, "I can never remember my dreams!" When you make these types of statements, you are coming into agreement with demonic forces to block that knowledge and revelation from God. Stop it now! Remember that death and life are in the power of the tongue (Proverbs 18:21). Pray and ask for spiritual assistance to be able to recall your dreams. Pray against forgetfulness, confusion, frustration and fatigue.

The memory of the righteous is blessed ...
Proverbs 10:7 NKJV

Here are a few Scriptures to recite before bed to increase the likelihood of remembering your dreams:
- Proverbs 3:24
- Psalm 4:8
- 2 Timothy 1:7
- James 4:7
- Jeremiah 31:26
- Psalm 91:1-5

- Proverbs 19:23
- Proverbs 6:22
- Psalm 121:5

TIME TO PRACTICE

Below is an actual dream that was recorded and is being used as an example of how to use the skills and tools discussed herein to begin the process of unlocking the mystery of your dreams.

June 30, 2019

I dreamed about hotels all night. In the first dream, I was in a large, luxurious hotel that we were staying in for a conference. Some of my students were there. The gentleman at the desk was supposed to give us a room on a higher floor, but then the shift changed. When I went to the front desk, a woman said they were preparing for something BIG and would not assist me. I went up to a higher floor to get assistance, but was escorted back to the stairs and directed elsewhere. (That floor could only be assessed by the stairs.)

I mentioned what I was going through to one of the conference attendees who accompanied me back to the front desk. She stood to the side and watched the interaction herself. Again, the ladies at the front desk looked at me and shook their heads like, "Nope, I'm busy." I had a clipboard in my hand, so I guess they didn't realize that I was a hotel guest. I asked to speak to management and explained what happened. As a result, I got a complimentary upgrade to their best suite.

Here is a recap of the steps to take to properly handle your dreams:

1. Revelation – The message is given in the form of a vision or dream (vision of the night). It has been released, but is not necessarily understood by the recipient.

2. Interpretation – You desire to know the meaning of the dream. The Holy Spirit can provide clarity and insight through the meanings of dream symbols and metaphors. It can come to the recipient directly or through someone with the gift of dream interpretation.

3. Application – What are you supposed to do with the message/communication? This is where additional prayer comes into play. Are

you to take action? Does something need to change? Are you to intercede on behalf of the person, the situation, etc.? These are the questions to ask once you have the interpretation. Remember that the great majority of dreams have personal revelation.

4. Proclamation – Are you supposed to tell anyone? Is this message specifically for you? Are you supposed to share outside of your personal dream journal? If so, determine not only who to share it with, but determine the proper timing, also.

As you review the dream, use different color highlighters or pens to distinguish the parts of the dream that answers the questions below.

Questions to Ask/Additional Steps to Take:

1. Who do you think is the source of the dream? God, Satan or self? Or was the dream based on interference?
   How did the dream make you feel when you woke up? This could be a clue to the source of the dream.

2. Pray for the proper interpretation of the dream if it is from God. Rebuke the dream and cancel any plots/schemes of the enemy if it is from Satan. If it is a fleshly or soulish dream, review your sleep hygiene and what you watch before going to sleep, then ignore the dream since it likely does not have a spiritual significance.

3. What is the symbolic language used? Underline, highlight or list specific dream symbols and their possible meanings.

4. Pull the meanings together in sentence form to see if you are able to gather a coherent message.

5. What type of dream is it? Review the list of *20 Types of Dreams* to see if it falls into one of these categories.

6. Who is the intended recipient of the dream? Is the dream personally for the dreamer or is the message intended for someone else?

7. What should you do with the information? If the message is for someone else, decide whether God wants you to pray for them, intercede for the situation or tell them as a warning.

For the sample dream that was given, the source of the dream was God. There was nothing indicated to think it was from Satan or self. The symbols in the dream that you could have underlined were hotel, conference, students, front desk, shift, interaction, clipboard, management, upgrade, suite.

- Hotel = temporary place
- Conference = dialogue, prayer or fellowship
- Students = schooling or learning
- Front desk = business or work issue
- Shift = transition/change
- Interaction (insincere) = heart not in it
- Clipboard = take notes/instruction
- Management = being in charge

- Upgrade =moving to another level/promotion
- Suite = before than (room) before

Every word underlined may not add to the interpretation, but it's best not to leave any major themes out, just in case. Upon looking up these symbols, along with prayer and seeking God, here is a possible interpretation:

You are in a temporary place. You may have had dialogue about what you have learned to date about work issues but a change is about to take place. You may have realized that those who were assigned to help you did not, or their heart wasn't in it. Take notes! The One who is in charge is moving you to another level. Promotion is coming and it is better than what was before.

This is quite likely a confirmation dream. It can be a confirmation since there is an obvious transition from being ignored and overlooked to receiving an upgrade. If this was something that the dreamer/recipient was already sensing in the spirit, then it is indeed a confirmation.

He will not let you fall; your protector is always awake.
Psalm 121:3 GNT

CHAPTER SIX

FINAL THOUGHTS

What are the goals of dreams? On the most simplistic level, dreams are to communicate from the spirit realm to us in the earth realm. On a deeper level, dreams are how spirits forge agreements and covenants to accomplish their will. In the same manner that God was able to bless people like Abraham and Solomon through dreams, dreams secure an agreement which either speaks for or against your future and destiny.

What have you come into agreement with during your dreams? What is in your life that's a violation of God's laws that you have given legal access to? If you do not resist the manifestation, then by default, you are inviting that "thing" to manifest in your life. That thing could be the spirit of poverty, spirit of delay, spirit of adultery, etc., along with the consequences written in the Word of God. God tries to protect us with His Word, but the enemy knows the Word and tries to use it against us. Read your Word daily so you are aware of the enemy's schemes.

Lest Satan should take advantage of us; for we are not
ignorant of his devices.
2 Corinthians 2:11 NKJV

We have taken this journey together through the night season, and now the dawn is upon us. Hopefully, you have gained some insightful tools to assist you with learning about the spirit realm, remembering your dreams and beginning to interpret your dreams so you know what steps you need to take in your waking hours. Dreams should not be interpreted in your intellect or through logic, but by the One who sent the dreams to you. Please do not try to receive spiritual communication without God.

Here is my closing prayer. It is a prayer that I often pray myself every morning when I awake. May the peace of God be yours both while you are awake and asleep.

Father God, I thank You for how You speak to me through my dreams. I welcome Your revelation and look forward to receiving from You as I sleep.

I repent for anything I have done that violates Your will, Your laws, Your principles or Your decrees. I come into alignment with Your will for my life.

I cancel every demonic agreement, every demonic covenant and destroy every evil altar in my life. I take every thought captive to the obedience of Christ Jesus, and submit to Your plan and purpose for my life in Jesus' name.

Holy Spirit, I welcome you. You are the great deliverer, Lord Jesus. You set the captives free. I call upon Your might; pull down and press into Your spirit of counsel and might (Isaiah 11: 2). Heavenly Father, I realize that I am in desperate need of deliverance in my spirit, my mind, my will and emotions – but specifically in my subconscious, my imagination, in my thinking and in my dream life.

Holy Spirit, I surrender and fully repent of opening the door to the demonic, willfully and ignorantly. Lord Jesus, I humbly ask You to set me free. Go into every room. Find every dark corner. Turn on all the lights. Expose all my graven images on the walls of my subconscious. Holy Spirit, I fully trust You right now to set me free.

Satan and every demon in my life, in my subconscious and in the area of my dreams, I command you — every terror by night, every incubus, succubus, spirit husband, spirit wife, sleep apnea, sleep paralysis, insomnia, nightmare demons and any other demon assigned to my dreams to loose me now, in Jesus' name.

In the name of Jesus Christ, leave my mind. Leave my soul. Leave my thinking. Leave my subconscious. Leave my dream life and leave my body now, in Jesus' name. I order you to pack your bags and leave me. Come out! Find your exit now in Jesus' name. AMEN.

References

1.   https://medalerthelp.org/blog/sleep-statistics/
2. Goll, James W., and Michal Ann Goll. *Dream Language: The Prophetic Power of Dreams, Revelations and the Spirit of Wisdom.* Destiny Image, Shippensburg, PA, 2006, p. 20.

Additional Acknowledgments

A special acknowledgment goes to my mommy, Gwen Lee, who first believed that I "learned things" in my dreams. I appreciate her support even when she did not fully understand the gift.

Almost 40 years ago, I met a young lady who has changed my life for the better. Neco Walker, you are my sister, the very best friend a girl could ask for and redefine the term "best friend forever". Thanks BFF!

To my bestie, my ride or die, Irel Broadnax, who always shows fierce love, ready to grab her boots and go to war, whether physically...or in the spirit. Thank you for not letting my tough exterior keep us from forming this lifetime bond.

Dr. Leah Robinson is a force to be reckoned with professionally and personally and I'm so glad she keeps pushing me to new heights and greater depths. Thank you for being on my squad!

To Tanya Michelle Vines, my other sister and childhood friend. Your family is my family. Regardless of what life throws our way, I'm here 'til the end.

To Denise Crumbey, one of the first people God allowed me to truly pour into as a mentor and friend. Having you in my life is an answered prayer in itself.

To Kashae Clegg, who has supported every one of my book projects and encourages me in countless ways. Thank you for holding me accountable, caring about my well-being and giving me a home away from home to visit.

To Mia Tillman, the one who has tugged on my gift of dream interpretation the most...I am so grateful that we crossed paths when we did. It is through your inquiries and messages that my first dream interpretation workshop and ultimately this book was birthed. You are a priceless gem in the Kingdom of God.

Finally, last but certainly not least, to Denise Shelton-Jackson, my lifelong friend...your presence in my life is irreplaceable. You mean more to me than you could ever know.

ADDITIONAL RESOURCES

The Bible will always be the best dream dictionary available; however, there are some pretty reliable sources:

The Divinity Code To Understanding Your Dreams and Visions
by Adam F. Thompson and Adrian Beale

Dream Language: The Prophetic Power of Dreams, Revelations and the Spirit of Wisdom by James W. and Michal Ann Goll

OTHER BOOKS BY THIS AUTHOR:

Fiction Titles by D. C. Wiggins

Their Darkest Hour

Almost Doesn't Count

If you have read any of these books, don't forget to leave a review!

Non-Fiction Titles by Dr. De'Andrea Matthews

The Overcomers' Anthology: Volume One

The Overcomers' Anthology: Volume Two – Overcoming Fear

The Published Professional:
Writing a Book to Build Your Brand (eBook only)

The Power of Prayer: An Anthology

Letters to My Angry Self: Unmasking a Lady of Rage

If you have read any of these books, don't forget to leave a review!

Other compilations featuring book chapters from
Dr. De'Andrea Matthews

Insights: The Proven Strategies for Success –
How Entrepreneurs Thrive in the Modern World
and How You Can Too by Antoine Airoldi

Campus Diversity Triumphs: Valleys of Hope (Diversity in
Higher Education) by Dr. Sherwood Thompson

Exploring Campus Diversity: Case Studies and Exercises by
Dr. Sherwood Thompson

Magnetic Entrepreneur:
My Success Formula by Robert J. Moore

Be sure to follow @drdcmatthews on social media. We'd love for you to post a photo of you holding your book for a special shout out!

https://www.youtube.com/c/DrDeAndreaMatthews

@drdcmatthews

@drdcmatthews

www.fb.me/drdcmatthews

https://drdcmatthews.wordpress.com/

ABOUT THE AUTHOR

Committed to edifying the kingdom of God, Dr. De'Andrea Matthews serves as senior pastor of Visions International Ministry where she teaches, trains and activates leaders to heal from trauma, experience victory over darkness and walk in their divine destinies. An international speaker and award-winning author, Dr. Matthews turned adversity into her advantage by showing others how to triumph over tragedy to become their greatest possible selves. Graced with an abundance of gifts and over twenty years of ministry experience, Dr. Matthews is paving the way for many to grow and thrive spiritually and professionally.

www.ingramcontent.com/pod-product-compliance
Lightning Source LLC
Chambersburg PA
CBHW071011120626
46546CB00003B/1040